First published in the UK in 2020 by
Tyne Bridge Publishing, City Library,
Newcastle-upon-Tyne, United Kingdom
www.tynebridgepublishing.org.uk
ISBN 13- : 978-1-8382809-0-1

The number of photographs allotted to each artist doesn't represent their importance. Also, due to the limited photographic material available from this period, we're aware that there are gaps. As an appendix, we've included a list of performers we wanted to include but were unable to contact.

We're very grateful to everybody who contributed. (Full credits on pages 96-97.)

All the writers' profits from this publication are to go to the Young Musicians Fund to develop the musical skills of children and young people who struggle to pay for tuition or need help to purchase an instrument.

Community **Foundation**
Tyne & Wear and Northumberland
Enriching lives through effective giving

More information at www.communityfoundation.org.uk/givingandphilanthropy/collective-giving/young-musicians-fund/

MiE Fielding is a Northumbrian artist ,writer, musician and producer. Further information at www.voert.digital

Simon McKay is the publisher of the music fanzine Eccentric Sleeve Notes and DJ for the online radio show 'Post Punk Britain'. He has written for Record Collector magazine and in 2017, with Fenella Fielding, wrote her autobiography 'Do You Mind If I Smoke?'

more at :
www.eccentricsleevenotes.com
www.soundcloud.com/postpunkbritain.

Introduction

1970s Britain experienced an unprecedented and seismic shift in music and culture. The decade that had started with the remnants of flower power and folk-rock, quickly worked its way through glam, soul, prog, blues, funk and jazz. These musical styles and the ubiquitous wearing of flared trousers would largely be blown away by the energy and DIY ethos of punk and new wave. This avalanche of creativity influenced the north east too and by the late 70s the region's pubs and clubs played host to a vast and exciting array of musical ideas and genres. Newcastle had a number of great venues, including the highly influential Spectro Arts Centre, the famous Victorian music hall Balmbra's, The Cooperage and others.

Just outside the city centre, The Gosforth Hotel, (which in earlier days was a regular venue for Sting and his jazz outfit 'Last Exit' pictured opposite), buzzed to the now legendary nights hosted by promoters Anti-Pop, and it was at these events that the people of Newcastle were introduced to the very first copies of the now internationally famous Viz comic.

Although the north east was particularly affected by Margaret Thatcher's cuts, the miners' strike and high unemployment, there were people willing to go out any night of the week. This created a wonderfully close and vibrant social scene that made Newcastle feel more like a village than a major city.

It's this late 1970s and up to mid-80s period we've tried to reflect with this photographic collection; particularly the increase in energy as punk, new wave and electronica caught hold. The new bands did not wipe out the established ones though, and we've included many who continued to attract large audiences while playing traditional genres like rock and blues.

We've presented the bands in photographs without offering any comment or critique. Some of the musicians would later enjoy major success, some became active in other artistic fields or in broadcasting. But what unites them all is that they were performing in Newcastle in an era that has to be the most creative in the city's illustrious history.

There were more changes by the mid-1980s. The venues, that had once hosted a plethora of punk and new wave bands, were slowly replaced by trendy new clubs and raves at unlicensed warehouses. The famous Balmbra's Music Hall closed. Spectro was demolished and many of the traditional pubs disappeared.

And that's pretty much where our story ends. This is the city we knew and loved and to paraphrase the 1985 Kane Gang chart hit, it's 'The Closest Thing to Heaven' *we* have ever known.

DUST

featuring a very young Neil Tennant (Pet Shop Boys) far left

GINNY OLIVER

7

TREATMENT ROOM

Eldon Square Free Festival

TREATMENT ROOM

WITH THE DEMCOX

AT THE GOLDEN FLEECE
(MARLBOROUGH BUS STN)
THURSDAY 2ND AUGUST
8.00 pm (ONLY 20p ON THE DOOR)

single out

AWAYDAY

Trea
tmen
troom

SHAPES

Gosforth Hotel

ANTS 'N' APHIDS
AWAY DAY ASSASSIN.
HUMAN MOSAICS
~~DOWN TO ATTACK~~.
DRIVING ROBOTS MAD
~~8 8~~
GARDENS OF SAND
FIGHT IGNORANCE
MENTAL MEN
BLIND IN A TOY SHOP
POP SONG.
(PILL BOX)

Treatment Room bass player Steve Oliver and, above, the set list

THE PRIZE GUYS

aka King Crabs

SNEEZE

STEVE BROWN BAND

PUNISHMENT OF LUXURY

Newcastle Guildhall, 1978

ROCK AGAINST RACISM

GUILDHALL NEWCASTLE
QUAYSIDE

THE BIG G

PUNISHMENT
OF LUXURY

PRESS STUDS ✳ ➤➤ ➤➤ SPEED &

DISCO

BAR   TICKETS 75p
            (40p WITH DOLE CARD)

THURSDAY NOVEMBER 24th 7·30–1·00

Rock Against Racism!

NEON

Neon

March 2 Polytechnic   Newcastle
      4   The Greyhound   London
      5   Golden Lion   London
      6   Bridge House   London
      7   Pegasus   London
      8   Nashville   London
      9   Railway Hotel   London
     10   Windsor Castle   Moonlight Club   London

Bright New Single **DON'T EAT BRICKS**
c/w HANGING OFF AN O

PENETRATION

14

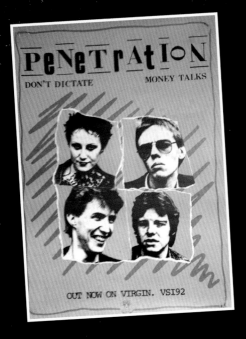

PENETRATION

DON'T DICTATE   MONEY TALKS

OUT NOW ON VIRGIN. VS192

new MUSICAL EXPRESS

JOHN
COOPER-CLARKE
Poetry in Motion P.7

CLASH
PERE UBU
Late Night Vinyl P.45

RESIDENTS
Leave Home P.12
Album Escapes P.51

BETHNAL
Greek Is The Word P.29

YES
A Good Laugh P.37

THE
PERILS
OF
PAULINE
P.38/39

listen ear

RECORDS
present
LIVE

GUILDHALL · NEWCASTLE
MONDAY · JUNE 6
7·30-1

ADVERTS
PENETRATION
HARRY HACK &
THE BIG G

BAR
CHEAP
FOOD
DISCO

75p

TICKET OUTLETS-
LISTEN EAR · VIRGIN · CALLERS
H.M.V. · C.A.T.S.U. · FRANKIE JOHNSON

THE NOISE TOYS

ANTI-POP ANTI-POP

SINGLE OUT NOW!

THE
Noise
Toys

the living
legend
ARTHUR 2 STROKE

AND Disorder all the
way from
Boldon

AT: GOSFORTH HOTEL (SALTERS ROAD)
ON: MONDAY 26th NOV. '79

HARRY HACK AND THE BIG G

THE WEIGHTS

19

MURDER THE DISTURBED

RAY STUBBS R&B ALLSTARS

THE SQUAD

NOD - PUNK POET

Daz gets you whiter than whiter than white
Daz makes you glow in the darkest of nights
Daz get your aura brighter than bright
Daz gets you faster faster than light
Stick some doon your neck get some up your nose
Daz gets you out there and it even cleans your clothes

Forces grey out and forces white in
Daz keeps your television free from sin
Daz Daz Daz Daz dripping down your chin
Daz to keep healthy Daz to keep you thin
Low in Carbohydrates less than slimming pills
Daz gets you out there, who need Chlorophyll

It's got blue Whitener to make you look good
It removes all the under stains and all the blood
Digests those things you shouldn't mention
Removes headaches relieves tension
Stick some under your armpits wash your intimate parts
Daz gets you out there and cleans out your heart

Two for one swap no thanks no thanks
Daz for H bombs Daz for tanks
Who needs to go to Afghanistan?
Daz for ayatollah's Daz is your man
Stick some in your bottle, pin it to your chest
Daz gets you out there cos it's better than the rest

Unfortunately some people are really thick
They use Omo! Say it does the trick
Well I ate some once it made us sick !
Killed a poor cat, he only had a lick
Stick with your Daz man, you'll be alright
Daz gets you there - smoke some tonight!

SPEED

THE PROLES

THE SABREJETS

WHITE HEAT

White Heat on a pre-pedestrianised Northumberland Street. This photograph was used as the single cover to "Nervous Breakdown" (page 79)

XEROX

Kings Head, Scotswood Road

Anti-Pop

Anti-Pop were a Newcastle-based independant label that promoted many local gigs.

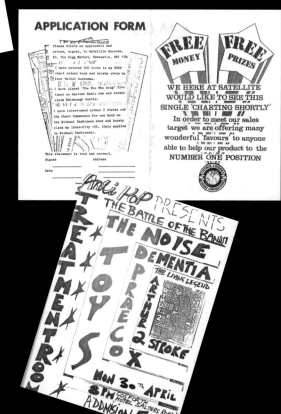

ARTHUR 2 STROKE

Would you give them your vote ??? !!

The M.P.s

MON. 8th MAY.
MON. 15th MAY : GOSFORTH HOTEL.
MON. 22nd MAY Supporting "SPEED" !!

THE MP'S

THE YOUNG BUCKS

Cooperage

JEFF JINX BAND

THE YELLOW JELLIES

PRAYER BEFORE BIRTH

THE CARPETTES

PHANTOMS OF THE UNDERGROUND

PHANTOMS OF THE UNDERGROUND
MATAMBA
THE EQUALISERS
GUILDHALL 17th JULY
ADM 1.00 7-12pm

DEMENTIA PRAECOX

Gosforth Hotel

38

DEMENTIA PRAECOX

Cooperage

SPARE PAIR

ANGELIC UPSTARTS

INSECURE

YOU ARE INVITED TO A CHRISTMAS PARTY WITH The Rhythm Methodists & insecure AT The GOLDEN FLEECE WESTMORLAND ROAD TUES. 16TH DEC 1980 9:30 – 10.45

TOTAL CHAOS   At the Garage

REPTILES   At the Garage

R&B SPITFIRES

Mayfair Ballroom Sunday Sur
'Night of Rock' in aid of the
Charlie Bear Scanner Appeal,
November 6, 1981.

THE FASHIONABLE IMPURE

The Delby Nightclub

BRIGHTON GROVE ALBION

THE FAUVES

MILAN STATION

JAZZAWAKI

DARKNESS & JIVE

44

PUNCHING HOLES

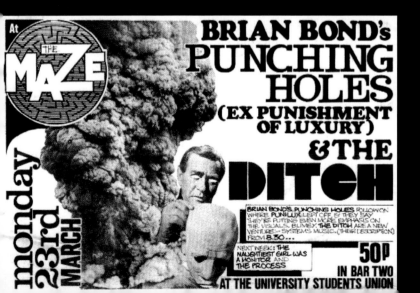

Stare crazy

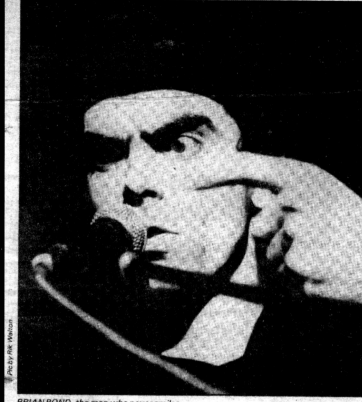

Pic by Rik Walton

BRIAN BOND, *the man who never smiles*

Punching Holes

Newcastle

PUNCHING HOLES are the unit assembled by Brian Bond after he vacated his position as Punishment of Luxury's frontman. The out and out theatrics of Punilux have been shunted to one side — no precision steps, silly suits or ski masks here — leaving Bond the Face to hold it all together.

As unconventional focus point, Bond could show certain neo-futurist pretenders a thing or two. The twists and turns of his gaunt chiselled features tell his manic tales as much as the voice does and seldom smiles, but is never sinister as this would be too easy a ploy for someone with such a strong face and piercing eyes to hide behind. He was totally convincing with Punilux and he's totally convincing with Punching Holes.

All of Holes' material is new (written largely by Brian and lead guitarist Tim Jones) with the exception of 'Damaging Man' which the Punishments played live and demoed but never put on record. What *is* carried over is the jagged jerky style. Holes are wayward ('Sour Faced Valerie' is even Zappaesque) and perhaps difficult to take in fully on one hearing. The exception is 'Crocodile Bird', a sort of male Lene Lovich effort, monks chanting and all.

The songs are demanding but with Brian Bond out front there's no way that Punching Holes are boring. They're a handful of gigs old and the muscians behind Bond are obviously still feeling him and each other out, but this is potentially a very stimulating combo.

IAN RAVENDALE

SHED

RAVEN

Pictured outside Spectro, Bells Court

46

ZOVIET FRANCE

VENOM

JU JU PELL MELL

(aka dumdum SCORE)

Cluny unlicensed event

VILLAGE IDIOTS

IAN BODDY

LAVERNE AND SHIRLIE

THE GROUND

TYGERS OF PAN TANG

DANCECLASS

The Tube

ACID

SCARED BANANAS

BLITZKRIEG BOP

54

EAST SIDE TORPEDOS

FEEBLE MINDED

JAYWALKERS

GOD'S GIFT TO WOMEN

ZAP

HOT LICKS COOKIES

57

SAID LIQUIDATOR

A VALENTINE
BLIND
DATE

WITH **SAID LIQUIDATOR**
AND LAVERNE & SHIRLIE
ROKEN DOLL • THURSDAY 14TH FEB • 8.30 • £1.50

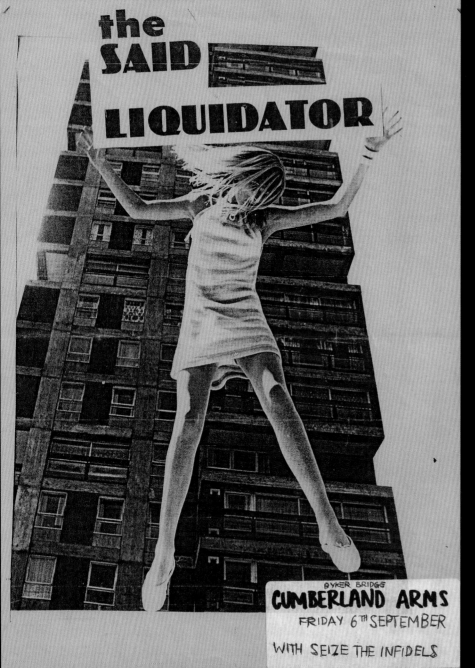

the SAID LIQUIDATOR

CUMBERLAND ARMS
FRIDAY 6TH SEPTEMBER

WITH SEIZE THE INFIDELS

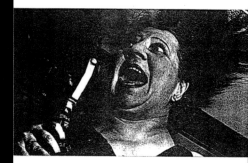

prefab sprout

The Militia Have Arrived!

The Monday Club
Tiffanys
Newcastle Upon Tyne
Monday 12th December
10.00pm to 2.00am
£1.00 Admission On The Door

PREFAB SPROUT

Prefab Sprout
sound checking
at Tiffanys

At Spectro Arts and (above) home made poster
for this gig

Prefab Sprout at the Lonsdale pub, Jesmond

Kitchenware Records

THE DAINTEES

hurraH
darkness & jive

KITCHENWARE

Tiffanys Tuesday 6th December
Tickets £2 *on the door ~ at record shops*
10pm to 3am £1.75 FOR ADVANCE, STUDENTS + UB40

why wait in by the phone ?

SOUL CELLAR HURRAH!
Downstairs at grey's club, grey st.
membership required

THURSDAY 21st APRIL 8-11

SOULED OUT !!
a guide to home taping soundslike
Hurrah!
Daintees
Prefab Sprout

KITCHENWARE *household goods*

(0632) 614874 / 710426

P.L.P. Present

Prefab Sprout

Plus Hurrah

NEWCASTLE MAYFAIR
THURS. 17th MAY 7.30
Tickets £3.50 from Box Office. Tel: 323109
and Virgin Records, HMV, Newcastle City Hall.

SUMMER SOUL

KITCHENWARE

Hurrah

YEM HOT 2
THE LOVETONES

FRI 29th JULY

AT THE COURTYARD
8 TRINITY CHARE
QUAYSIDE

· STRENGTH FOR OTHERS! ·   8-12 LATE BAR £1·00

Newcastle-based Kitchenware Records was founded in 1982 by Keith Armstrong, Paul Ludford and Phil Mitchell. They were very selective about the local bands they signed. Their roster included Hurrah!, The Daintees, Prefab Sprout and The Kane Gang.

THE DAINTEES

THE SOUL KITCHEN presents

NEW SOUNDS NEW HOPE NEWCASTLE!!

HURRAH!

the DAINTEES

tiffanys thurs 17 june
tickets £1·50 HMV VOLUME VIRGIN   8-2
pm am

participate & be....THE SOUL KITCHEN DISCO

THE KANE GANG

Back stage at Newcastle City Hall with Keith Armstrong (Kitchenware), Paddy McAloon (Prefab Sprout) and Tom Robinson (far left)

Kane Gang on stage at Newcastle City Hall with Paul Weller on congas, Mike Talbot on Keys, and Steve White on drums (The Style Council).

HURRAH!

68

The Venues

The Gosforth Hotel

The Mayfair Ballroom

Rockshots

The Cooperage

Walkers

Bridge Hotel

The King's Head

The Lonsdale

Broken Doll

Red House

TIFFANYS
~ PRESENT ~
Newcastles most
fashionable club
A
PACKET OF
CORNFLAKES
disko
wednesdays
only 75
9:00
2:00

The
Jewish
Mother

Balmbra's Music Hall

Tiffany's

Newton Park

Barley Mow

The Guildhall

The Golden Fleece

The Durham Ox

Egypt Cottage

The Baltic

Tyne Tees Television

The Tube

Jools Holland introduces 'The Tube' from Studio 5, Tyne Tees Television, City Road, Friday 5th November 1982.

The Shops

Callers was one of the city's main music stores.

Top left, the wonderful Handyside Arcade. Above, 'Fynd'. Left, 'Kard Bar' and right, 'Volume Records', Ridley Place.

Singles

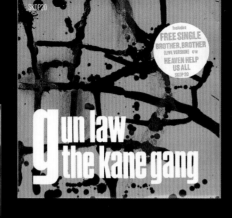

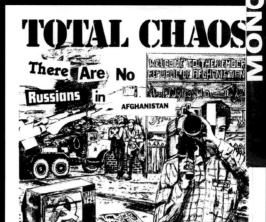

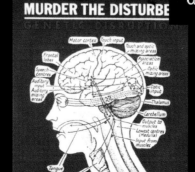

Artwork

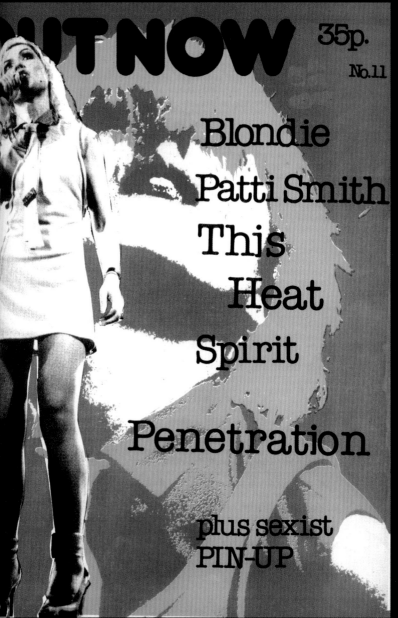

OUT NOW 35p.

No.11

Blondie
Patti Smith
This
Heat
Spirit

Penetration

plus sexist
PIN-UP

Thé Fàshionäbl Impure

spectro sat. aug. 8

MILAN STATION

NEW

FEBRUARY FRI. 13TH / SAT. 16TH

GIVE YOURSELF
A LIFT

AT

TIFFANYS

on

Tues. 6th Dec. 1983

10.00pm – 3.00am

with

Darkness
+
Jive

Hurrah

THE DAINTEES

£1.75 STUDENTS, UB40 OR ADVANCE.

OTHERS £2.00 ON THE DOOR.

Tickets – Volume, Virgin, or Windows

KITCHENWARE RECORDS Good Clean Fun....

CABARET
ROCKSHOTS
SUNDAY 22ND SEPT.
7.30PM–10.30PM

VIDEOS · DISCO

NICO
+ THE FACTION

GUESTS
PAPERWALLS
SEIZE THE INFIDELS

TICKETS:
ADVANCE £3.00
DOOR £3.50
VIRGIN VOLUME
PET SOUNDS
LP CAMERA OBSCURA PRODUCED
BY · JOHN CALE

electronic disco and

Dépôt Delby

sat 26 Feb
2.00 close
admission 1 pound

NEON
SQUAD
DISGUISE
TREATMENT ROOM
AT THE
NEWCASTLE MAYFAIR
THURSDAY 1st FEB
1979

FROM 7·30 UNTIL 1·0 AM
NO DRESS RESTRICTIONS
+ DISCO

TICKETS £1·60 FROM Colleges, Listen Ear, Musicore

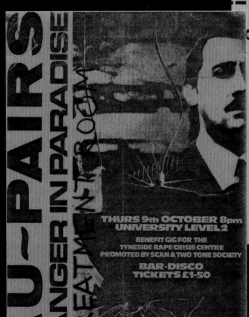

AU-PAIRS
DANGER IN PARADISE
TREATMENT ROOM

THURS 9th OCTOBER 8pm
UNIVERSITY LEVEL 2
BENEFIT GIG FOR THE
TYNESIDE RAPE CRISIS CENTRE
PROMOTED BY SCAN & TWO TONE SOCIETY
BAR·DISCO
TICKETS £1·50

SEIZE THE INFIDELS

the SAID LIQUIDATOR

8pm. redhouse 60p

MONDAY CLUB PRESENT!
Hurrah
AT TIFFANYS FUNCTION SUITE
MONDAY 8th AUGUST
9·00pm–1·00am
plus
alternative
disco

THE WILLUS B
At The Kings Head
live at 8pm
Feb 29??

JU-JU
ALL - MELI

Live at The
DELBY
ghost band
The strict baptists
EXTRAS
painful decisions

FRIDAY
20th FEB
8pm–2am
late bar

THE MONDAY CLUB
PRESENT!
THE
DAINTEES
AT TIFFANYS FUNCTION SUITE
MONDAY 15th AUGUST
9·00pm–1·00am
plus alternative disco

JU+JU

Monday 1st July, 1985
Riverside
Plus "The Said Liquidator"

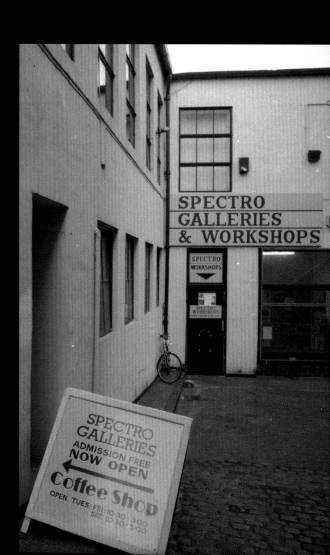

Spectro Arts Workshop (later Newcastle Media Workshop) was established to house a visual arts gallery, private studios, electronic music studio, a performance space, a screenprint studio and a photographic workshop. In addition there was a bar and cafe. It became one of the most influential and important hubs in the city for those involved in the creative arts.

Rock Against Racism

The Guildhall, 1979

Getting Out!

Music lovers made their way to the city's music venues and shops by bus, train and the Metro, below, which opened in August 1980.

Marlborough Crescent bus station

Worswick Street bus station and (below) Haymarket Station

The People

Adam Ant (Below) and The Jam (top right) at Listen Ear record shop.

Photo credits and further reading

Inset :	Sting and Last Exit, courtesy of Ronnie Pearson.
Page 6, 7	Dust & Ginny Oliver, coutesy of David M James.
Page 8, 9:	Treatment Room, courtesy of Chris Simpson.
Page 10:	Treatment Room, courtesy of Ed Hayes.
Page 11:	The Prize Guys & Sneeze, courtesy of www.readysteadygone.co.uk.
Page 11:	Steve Brown, courtesy www.sbb73to78.wordpress.com.
Page 12:	Punishment of Luxury, courtesy of Brian Bond www.facebook.com/punilux.
Page 13 :	Neon, courtesy of Tim Jones www.aural-innovations.com/stonepremonitions/bands/neon/
Page 14,15:	Penetration, courtesy of Brian Gibson www.briangibson.yolasite.com more at http://penetrationband.com.
Page 16,17:	The Noise Toys, courtesy of Voert Digital.
Page 18:	Harry Hack & The Big G, courtesy of Brian Gibson www.briangibson.yolasite.com.
Page 19:	The Weights, courtesy of Ed Hayes.
Page 20.	Red Performance, courtesy of Ed Hayes.
Page 21:	Murder The Disturbed, courtesy of www.facebook.com/pages/category/Musician-Band/Murder-the-Disturbed-269991386452708.
Page 21:	The Squad, courtesy of www.johnefarmer.com/page16.html.
Page 21:	Ray Stubbs, courtesy of Rik Walton photography www.rikwalton.com.
Page 22:	Nod, courtesy of Alan Clark..
Page 23:	Speed & The Proles, courtesy of Brian Gibson www.briangibson.yolasite.com.
Page 24 :	Monoconics, courtesy of Denny Pooley.
Page 25:	The Sabrejets, courtesy of Rik Walton photography www.rikwalton.com.
Page 26, 27:	White Heat, courtesy of Rik Walton photography www.rikwalton.com.
Page 28, 29:	The Willus Bnad, courtesy of Ed Hayes.
Page 30:	Xerox, courtesy of Ed Hayes.
Page 32, 33:	Arthur 2 Stroke, courtesy of www.voert.digital.
Page 34:	The MP's, courtesy of Brian Gibson www.briangibson.yolasite.com.
Page 35:	The Young Bucks, courtesy of Rik walton photography www.rikwalton.com.
Page 38:	Dementia Praecox, courtesy of www.voert.digital.
Page 39:	Dementia Praecox, (Steve Savage) www.voert.digital/.
Page 39:	Spare Pair, courtesy of Ed Hayes.
Page 40:	Angelic Upstarts, courtesy of Rik walton photography www.rikwalton.com.
Page 41:	Insecure courtesy of David Rigg.
Page 41:	Total Chaos & Reptiles at The Garage courtesy Simon McKay www.eccentricsleevenotes.com.
Page 42:	R&B Spitfires, courtesy of Charlie Bear Scanner Appeal.
Page 43:	Fasionable Impure, courtesy of Chris Simpson.

LINDISFARNE

Newcastle City Hall, Christmas 1976

Below is a list of bands that we remember fondly. Unfortunately, we were unable to obtain photographs of them in time for this book's publication.

The Adventures of Twizzle, All Because The Lady Loves, The Architects, Block Brothers, Chunkheads, Cube, Danger in Paradise, Dutch, Extras, 40 Men, The Funeral Directors, The Game, Ghost Band, Hostages, In Crowd, Junco Partners (reformed in 1977), Made in England, Model Workers, Music Like Dirt, Nothing, Painful Decision, Parting Shots, Perfect Crime, Pin up, Pleasure Bureau, Quinn the Eskimo, The Presidents, Rhythm Methodists, Risetime, Sher Khan, The Spares, Strength, The Surge, 21 Strangers, Uproar, V Corporation, The Word and finally our old mate Buzzin Willie from Wallsend (lights).